ABOVE: Women playing medieval frame drums, engraving. Rhythm has been with us since the beginning. It was the Greek philosopher Pythagoras [570–490 BCE] who realised that musical harmony unfolds via the very same simple ratios as rhythm, the octave 2:1, the fifth 3:2 and the fourth 4:3, ratios which also appear in fine art and architecture, nature, and, for Pythagoras, cosmology.

US edition © 2025 by Julian Gerstin
Published by Wooden Books LLC,
San Rafael, California

First published in the UK in 2024
by Wooden Books LTD, Glastonbury

Library of Congress Cataloging-in-Publication Data
Gerstin, J.
Rhythm

Library of Congress Cataloging-in-Publication
Data has been applied for

ISBN-10: 1-952178-48-7
ISBN-13: 978-1-952178-48-1

All rights reserved
For permission to reproduce any part of this
rhythmic little book please contact the publishers

Designed and typeset by Wooden Books, Glastonbury, UK

Printed in India on FSC® certified papers by
Quarterfold Printabilities Pvt. Ltd.

RHYTHM
PATTERN IN TIME

Julian Gerstin

with Brian Shankar Adler, George Howlett & Robin Tyndale-Biscoe

To Ken Dalluge, my brother in rhythm.

THANKS to Brian Shankar Adler, George Howlett, and Robin Tyndale-Biscoe for their assistance, to Ken Dalluge for ideas and arguments, and to John Martineau and Matt Tweed at Wooden Books for editing and knowledge. FURTHER READING: John Miller Chernoff *African Rhythm and African Sensibility*, Johnny Farraj & Sami Abu Shumays *Inside Arabic Music*, Rebeca Mauleón *Salsa Guidebook*, Various *The Garland Encyclopedia of World Music*.

Patterns and rhythm are everywhere in nature. They unfold in time: seasons, tides, the orbiting planets, generations of living beings, the muscular pulsations of our heart, the electric impulses of our neurons. They unfold in shapes: flowers, spider webs, crystals, cracks in dried mud. We perceive them even when they are impossible to pin down: the fractal branching of trees, the tumultuous layering of clouds, or the swirl of a flock of birds, all unpredictable yet there. ABOVE: Japanese Fabric Pattern, based on The Great Wave Off Kanagawa, by Hokusai [1760–1849]. PAGE VI: Prosobranchia by Ernst Haeckel [1834–1919].

CONTENTS

Introduction	1
Beats & Subdivisions	2
Measures	4
Meter	6
On & Off the Beat	8
More Suspension	10
Reggae, Samba, & Choro	12
Asymmetry & 3-3-2	14
3-3-2 Variations	16
Reggaetón & Bhangra	18
Building with 3-3-2	20
Guide Patterns	22
Offset Rhythms & Gamelan	24
Swing & Jazz	26
Funk	28
Motown, Rock, & Punk	30
Hip-Hop, D&B, & Trap	32
Polyrhythm	34
More Polyrhythm	36
Further Polyrhythm	38
Polymeter	40
Uneven Beats & Odd Meters	42
Iqa'at Cycles	44
Middle Eastern Rhythms	46
North Indian Rhythm	48
Tala Variations	50
Carnatic Rhythm	52
Repetition & Variation	54
Musical Form	56
Appendix: Western Rhythmic Notation	58

Introduction

Rhythm is pattern. Pattern is rhythm. Our bodies make rhythm: heartbeats, breathing, walking, running, sex, dance. The slow rhythms of waking and sleeping, digestion, the growth of cells. The long rhythm of life, its growth and decline. Our minds make rhythm. We see patterns in nature. We discover patterns in numbers. We observe the growth of plants, the crash and slosh of ocean waves, the cycles of the Sun, Moon and planets. Our senses take in the world's explosion of colors, sounds and movement, and our mind shapes these into things we recognize, relationships we understand. This is how we create meaning: through patterns, through rhythm. No wonder that rhythm is a primary aspect of music: for us humans, it's a fundamental part of the way we perceive and make sense of the world.

Some aspects of musical perception appear to be innate. Most human cultures perceive the correspondence between a note and its twin an octave higher, and most cultures can keep a steady beat, but there is also much in music that is specific to particular styles and groups of people—cultural and historical meanings layered right down to the level of perception, what you *hear*. When European travelers first encountered African drumming, they were simply unequipped to comprehend its patterns, and dismissed it as barbaric, rather than the complex and sophisticated art it is. Indian listeners hear nuances of emotion in raga that most Westerners just don't catch. This book includes examples of rhythms from many cultures. Each really deserves its own book, but I hope these quick glimpses will nevertheless give you a sense of the variety of ways in which people create musical rhythm.

BEATS & SUBDIVISIONS
and representing them

When you walk, you probably keep a fairly steady pace of even footsteps (*below*). In music these are BEATS, usually a steady series of discrete sounds around the pace of walking, jogging, or your heartbeat. If you find yourself tapping your foot or clapping along to music, that's probably the beat (or 'pulse'). Much of the world's music has steady, even beats, good for dancing, physical labor, marching, and other types of movement. They are a solid framework to hang other sounds on.

If musical rhythm were nothing more than a line of beats, it would soon get boring. Almost all musical styles add notes in between the beats: SUBDIVISIONS. Try keeping a steady beat with your foot, and clap the subdivisions between one beat and the next (*opposite*).

Worldwide, the most common subdivisions are 2, 3, or 4 notes per beat (including the beat itself). The beats are numbered one, two, and so on, to help musicians keep track of which beat is which, and where they are in the pattern. Slicing the beat into two (or four) small notes is BINARY subdivision; into three small notes, TERNARY subdivision.

TEMPO refers to the music's speed (beats per minute), but don't confuse it with fast notes like 16ths or 32nds. When musicians talk about the tempo of a piece of music, they're thinking of the main beats, which are usually at a pace your body can relate to easily. Subdivisions slice up the beats, but they don't change the underlying tempo.

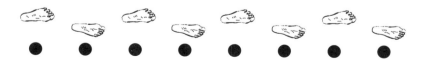

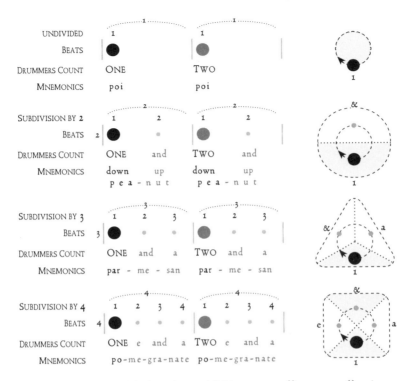

ABOVE: **BEATS** and the three primary subdivisions, BINARY (2), TERNARY (3) and QUATERNARY (4). To represent them in this book we will mainly use a dot system (where every dot gets the same amount of time), along with the **DRUMMER'S COUNT** (pronounced *"one ee and ah two ee and ah"*) and mnemonics like *"peanut"*. Rhythmic patterns can also be represented as wheels. Some notes are shown smaller and paler. These are **RESTS**, where you don't play. But they are still there, occupying time. To play the examples, say all the notes, but clap only on the larger, darker ones.

MEASURES
grouping the beats

Subdivisions are smaller than beats; now we need something larger.

When we start counting beats, we could in theory keep going forever: *one, two, three, four, five ... one hundred ninety-eight, one hundred ninety-nine ...* but this would be rather awkward. Instead, in music, beats are usually grouped together in short cycles.

For example, each phrase of Twinkle Twinkle Little Star has four beats (*see opposite top*). Notice the rests after "star" and "are", on beat 4. You need to honor these spaces, even though you don't sing on them. Rests give rhythms moments to breathe—literally breathe, when you're singing. Repeating cycles like these are called MEASURES.

In written music, measures are marked off by vertical BAR LINES, so they are also called BARS (*see opposite*). Beat 1, the first beat of the bar, is called the DOWNBEAT. Sometimes words or music start before the downbeat and lead into it; these are PICK-UPS. In Hard Day's Night, "It's been a" leads to "hard" on the first downbeat (*see below*).

Beats, subdivisions of the beat, beats grouped into measures: these are three basic levels of rhythmic organization in most of the world's music. However, this way of presenting the basics is still rather Western-oriented, not universal. In the section on Hindustani music, we'll see a different approach to these basics. Such differences are an exciting part of music, and of the diversity of human experience.

HAPPY BIRTHDAY, trad.	HARD DAY'S NIGHT, The Beatles, 1964
Happy | BIRTH - *day*	*It's been a* | HARD
PICK-UP | DOWNBEAT	PICK-UP | DOWNBEAT

ABOVE: Subdivisions in Western notation. You can slice them up further, but it's decorative, not rhythmic.

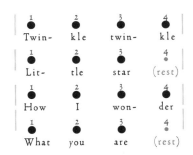

LEFT: The children's song Twinkle Twinkle Little Star has four beats in each line or bar, with rests on beat 4 of every other line. Each line forms a measure. Rests punctuate the rhythm and allow the singer to breathe. Try skipping them by running "little star how I wonder" together, and see what happens. This melody was developed in the 1780s by Wolfgang Amadeus Mozart from an old French nursery song, and the lyrics were written in 1806 by English poet Jane Taylor.

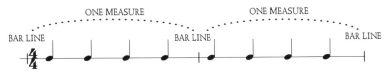

ABOVE: **MEASURES**. Here there are four quarter notes in each bar. We take some beats, subdivide them, and then group them into measures to form a rhythmic structure.

ABOVE: **TIME SIGNATURES** (the figures at the beginning of a piece of music that look like fractions) give information needed for writing and reading Western notation. The bottom number tells you what type of note to count; the top number tells you how many of that note are in a measure.

METER
combining the levels

The elemental numbers used in musical rhythm, pretty much everywhere in the world, are 2, 3, and 4. These are small units, easily perceived and easily manipulated. You can repeat them for larger units: 2, 4, 8, 16, 32 or 3, 6, 12. As the numbers get larger your mind tracks the small units inside them; whether you're aware of it or not, you sense four 4s in 16, four 8s in 32.

When you combine 2, 3, or 4 beats with subdivision by 2, 3, or 4, you create some of the world's most common rhythmic schemes. These combinations are **METERS**, which, generally speaking, means *how many beats + how they are subdivided* (*see opposite top*).

A well-known song should make meter clearer. Below we can see that *Jingle Bells* has phrases of four beats, subdivided by two. In the first two phrases all the words are on beats, so you might wonder why there are subdivisions; it's because "the", in the third bar, requires them. Also note that when you sing "way" you don't cut it short; you hold it for at least a full beat. Melodic notes have **DURATION**, which is an important part of rhythm. However, in this book, we will be mostly concerned with where notes begin (their **ATTACK**), not where they end. Other examples are shown (*opposite*).

●	●	●	●		●	●	●	●	
Jin -	gle	bells			Jin -	gle	bells		
1 and	2 and	3 and	4 and		1 and	2 and	3 and	4 and	
down up	down up	down up	down up		down up	down up	down up	down up	

●	●	●	●	●				
Jin -	gle	all		the	way			
1 and	2 and	3 and	4 and		1 and	2 and	3 and	4 and
down up	down up	down up	down up		down up	down up	down up	down up

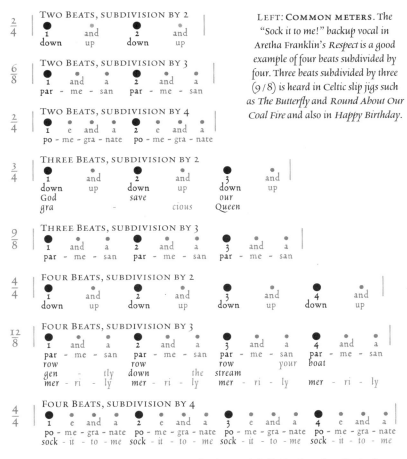

LEFT: **COMMON METERS**. The "Sock it to me!" backup vocal in Aretha Franklin's *Respect* is a good example of four beats subdivided by four. Three beats subdivided by three (9/8) is heard in Celtic slip jigs such as *The Butterfly* and *Round About Our Coal Fire* and also in *Happy Birthday*.

ABOVE: *Row, Row, Row Your Boat* uses four beats, subdivided in threes (12/8). The first two lines, "Row, row, row your boat/Gently down the stream", are mainly on the beat and only hint at the subdivisions. But they become obvious with "merrily...". The sound of three beats divided in twos (3/4) is heard in waltzes, and in *God Save the Queen* (*My Country 'Tis of Thee* in the US), where all the notes are on the beat except "-cious", which comes on the "and" after beat 2.

ON & OFF THE BEAT
grounding and suspension

What does it actually *feel* like to be on or off the beat, or on one beat rather than another, or on a particular note off the beat? Try stepping on a beat (or tapping your foot) and clapping along with your steps (*opposite, a*). Easy! The beats feel solid and grounded. Now try stepping on the beat and clapping all the binary subdivisions (*opposite, b*). This is FLOW. At a moderate tempo, a flow of notes often creates a sense of ease, like water rippling over rounded stones in a stream. Baroque music is full of flow (*see Hayden, p.13*). At a faster tempo the same structure can be driving—listen to the drum breaks in The Surfaris' 1963 hit W*ipeout*.

When you walk, you pick your feet up and put them down again. Your steps are beats and the lifts in between them are *and*s (which musicians call OFFBEATS). Try walking, and as you lift your feet, halfway between your steps, clap (*opposite, c*). This is why we use the mnemonic *down up*. Beats are rhythmically GROUNDED and *and*s are rhythmically SUSPENDED. Playing notes off the beat is called SYNCOPATION. Syncopation is what you do, suspension is how it feels.

Suspension creates excitement. When you dance, it is the lift of your foot, the shifting of weight. Many styles of dance music around the world feature offbeat *and*s. DOUBLE OFFBEATS subdivide by four and add a note, making "*and a*" (*see examples opposite*).

We Will Rock You, Brian May, 1977

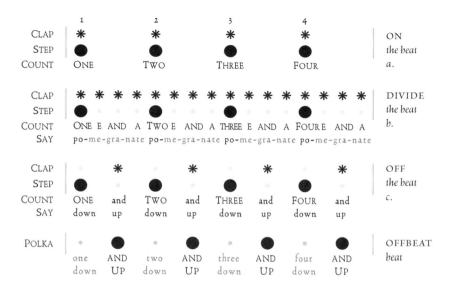

ABOVE: *From beats to offbeats ("and"s). The offbeat polka pattern is also the conga or shaker pattern in the CUMBIA rhythm of Columbia.* BELOW: *Some examples of "and a" double offbeats.*

FACING PAGE: *Offbeats feature in melody as well. In Brian May and Queen's We Will Rock You, every note of the refrain squats squarely on the beat, until the last word, "you", catches you off guard and pulls you up into suspension. Try singing the refrain with "you" on beat 2 instead. Boring! Had the song been written like that, it would never have been a hit.*

More Suspension
grounding the backbeat

In the Western classical tradition, beat 1 (the DOWNBEAT) is considered the strongest, and beat 3 the second strongest (*opposite, a*). The opposite is true in rock, funk, and hip-hop, where beats 2 and 4, the BACKBEAT, are emphasised. (*opposite, b*). Originally played on snare drum (e.g. Sly & the Family Stone's Thank You (*Falettinme Be Mice Elf Agin*)), the backbeat might be combined with handclaps (Parliament Funkadelic's One Nation Under a Groove), synthesizer (Grandmaster Flash & the Furious Five's The Message), or tamborine (Junior Walker & the All Stars' Shotgun).

The backbeat has been ubiquitous in popular music for over fifty years. If you've ever wondered why, now you know: backbeats are grounded and steady because they're beats, but at the same time, compared to the relatively inert beats 1 and 3, they're active and dynamic.

Es and As are a higher level of suspension. Try stepping on the beat (or tapping your foot) while clapping *e*s and *a*s (*opposite, c*). You may very well find that your claps slide down onto the beat without your noticing. Beats have gravity; they pull you down. The further you go up the levels of subdivisions, the more unbalanced but exciting the music feels. Subdivisions are tension, beats are resolution.

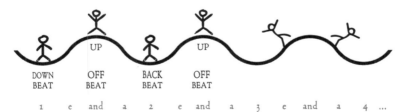

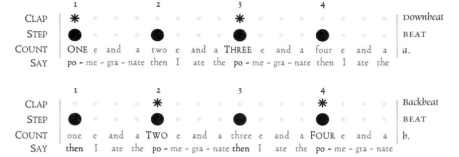

ABOVE: Western theory considers the DOWNBEAT (beat 1) and beat 3 the strongest, but this gets flipped in rock and funk, where the BACKBEAT, beats 2 and 4, are emphasised.

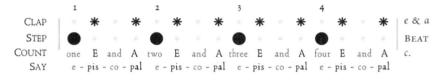

ABOVE: As offbeats are to beats, so Es and As are to both beats and offbeats: another layer slid in between. They are precarious but exciting, the steep sides of the hills (see opposite).

Opening of Franz Josef Hayden, Sonata HOB No.1 in C Major

ABOVE: A passage of flowing Baroque music (see. p.10), with the left hand playing all divisions, 1 e & a, etc. FACING PAGE: Picture beats as the valleys in a landscape. "And"s are the hills between them. When you clap the "and"s, you're balancing on the top of the hill. This is relatively steady compared to "e"s and "a"s. With "e"s and "a"s you're on the side of the hill; it's icy and slippery, and you have to work just to keep your balance.

Reggae, Samba, & Choro
masterclasses in suspension

Reggae is a great example of suspension. It travels across the hills (*see p.10*), on backbeats, on offbeat *and*s, and on highly suspended *e*s and *a*s.

In a typical reggae song, you'll hear a solid thud on beats 2 and 4, like the snare drum backbeats in funk (*p.28*) and rock (*p.30*), but on the drummer's bass drum (*opposite top*). This is called the ONE DROP, and it creates suspension down in the very foundation of the groove. The rhythm guitar plays offbeat *and*s. Strumming a chord on *and* is SKANK, while doubling it (*and a*) is DOUBLE CHOP. Up on the *e*s and *a*s is the BUBBLE, played on a keyboard. These notes surround the offbeat (though sometimes the keyboardist adds the offbeat as well). The keyboard sound is usually lighter than the rhythm guitar, and adds a floating quality to the music; you might call it a gentle high.

Brazilian music also glories in suspension. The Carnival music of Rio de Janeiro is played by SAMBA schools of up to 300 percussionists. Bass drums lay a foundation of backbeats while shakers and snare drums add flow, which swings in a characteristically Brazilian way (*see p.26*). Bells, small drums and other instruments play patterns like TELECOTECO, dancing around the beat with a flurry of highly suspended *e*s and *a*s (*see opposite*). The three elements—beats, flow, suspension—combine into highly exciting, yet coherent, music.

Another Brazilian music style is Choro, which developed in Rio c.1870. It uses a wide variety of rhythms (*see example below*).

Choro	✱ ✱ ✱ ✱ ✱ ✱ ✱ ✱ ✱
	1 e & a 2 e & a 3 e & a 4 e & a
	dig it - I dig it - I dig it - I dig it - I

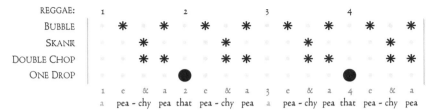

ABOVE: REGGAE. For SKANK, listen to Dawn Penn's *No No No*. For DOUBLE CHOP, Bob Marley's *Sun Is Shining*. You can hear the BUBBLE on Gregory Isaac's *Nightnurse*.

ABOVE: In SAMBA, bass drums play beats and backbeats, shakers and snares add flow, and high percussion plays suspended patterns like telecoteco and its variants. Variation 1 is telecoteco with two notes omitted. Variation 2 is a 10-click rotation of the original (see p.15). Note: Brazilian musicians count in 2/4, so here we show two measures of two beats each.

FACING PAGE: CHORO is classically played on acoustic instruments and has a light rhythmic feel. Central to that feel is an accompaniment that may be played on any instrument (guitar, piano, flute, pandeiro) featuring bubbly "e"s and "a"s anchored by the beat. This pattern is called GARFINHO, "little fork", because the three notes with the beat in the middle look like the tines of a fork. The bass introduction to the Temptations' *My Girl* is the same pattern.

ASYMMETRY & 3-3-2
the ancient rhythm

So far, our patterns have mostly been evenly spaced. Now let's mix things up a bit, and carve time into some interesting, jagged shapes.

The 3-3-2 pattern is one of the most important rhythms in the world, and is probably quite ancient. It appears throughout Africa, and travelled from there to the Caribbean and South America. It surrounds the Mediterranean from Greece through Turkey and the Levant, and all across North Africa. You hear it in the Balkans and Central Asia, India and Pakistan, Indonesia, and even in folk music from Vietnam, Korea, and Japan. As a fundamental pattern in African music it has become an essential part of virtually every Caribbean style—salsa (*p.9*), reggaetón (*p.18*), mambo (*p.22*), calypso, soca (*p.17*), zouk—and of every US popular style from ragtime and jazz to rock (*p.30*), funk (*p.28*), and hip hop (*p.32*).

The pattern has different names in different languages. It is TRESILLO in Spanish-speaking Latin America, BHAJANI in Hindustani India, ČOČEK in Macedonia and Bulgaria, NIM SOFYAN in Turkey, MALFUF and WAHDA in the Arabic world, IKWOKORIKWO in the Urhobo language of Eastern Nigeria, and many more. We call it 3-3-2. This refers to its groups of three, three, and two subdivisions, as shown in the count: 1 2 3 1 2 3 1 2 and the mnemonic: ***par**-me-san **par**-me-san **pea**-nut*.

THE 3-3-2 RHYTHM	GROUPS	⌒3⌒	⌒3⌒	⌒2⌒
		1 - 2 - 3	1 - 2 - 3	1 - 2
	3-3-2	● · ·	● · ·	● ·
	COUNT	ONE e and	A two e	AND a
	MNEMONICS	par-me-san	par-me-san	pea-nut

ABOVE: The 3-3-2 rhythm is struck on a bell in the KINKA dance of the Ghanaian Ewe people. It is also the snare drum in The Meters' *Hey Pocky Way*, the keyboard in Coldplay's *Clocks*, and the bass in the Wild Tchoupitoulas' *Brother John* and The Meters' *Mardi Gras Mambo*.

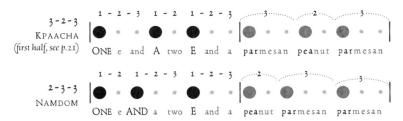

ABOVE: Two more bell patterns from traditional dances of the Ewe people show how the 3-3-2 pattern can also be reconfigured as 3-2-3 or 2-3-3. That said, the 3-3-2 order is especially powerful because the second note anticipates beat 2 on the precarious slope of the hill, and the third note is an offbeat, keeping dancers on their feet.

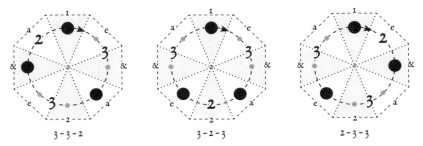

ABOVE: The 3-3-2 (or 1-2-3 1-2-3 1-2) rhythm and its ROTATIONS shown as a wheel, with beat 1 at the top. Other rotations which do not start on the beat are possible, such as a gongue (bell) pattern from maracatu music of NE Brazil (3 1-2-3 1-2 1-2), bell patterns from Eastern Caribbean carnival styles (3 1-2 1-2-3 1-2), and a danmyé variation from Martinique (2 1-2-3 1-2-3 1).

3-3-2 Variations
habanera, soca and cinquillo

3-3-2 is such a vivid pattern that it often appears in other guises and still maintains its identity. To begin exploring, let's add a single note on beat 2 (*below*). This variation is as ancient as 3-3-2 itself and is heard in many traditional styles. For instance, the KINKA dance of the Ghanaian Ewe people includes a rattle shaken downwards and upwards, with 3-3-2 in the downstrokes and beat 2 on the up (*opposite top*). In the 1800s, this rhythm became widely known as HABANERA ("of Havana"), and anchored a dance of the same name. Though the pattern is old, it continues to fuel modern dance music: it is a staple of reggaetón (*p.20*), Trinidadian soca (*opposite*), Balkan brass bands (Boban Markovic's Mundo Čoček), Arabic pop (Hakim's AhYa Albi), Bollywood songs (Dekhte Dekhte, Dilbar), and other styles around the world.

Add two notes to 3-3-2 and you get patterns known in Latin America as CINQUILLO ("five notes", *lower opposite*). Cinquillos are found throughout African-influenced music of the Caribbean. Cinquillo A, for instance, is played with sticks on wood or bamboo to accompany both Puerto Rican BOMBA and the BÈLÈ of Martinique. Cinquillo B is one half of the basic rhythm of Cuban DANZÓN. These variations were vital to the popular dance styles that emerged in the rapidly growing cities of Latin America in the late 19th and early 20th centuries, such as Argentinean TANGO.

3-3-2	• . . • . . • . | • . . . • . • .	ONE e and A two e AND a parmesan parmesan peanut
HABANERA	● . . ● ● . . ● . | ● . . . ● ● . ● .	ONE e and A TWO e AND a parmesan peppermint peanut

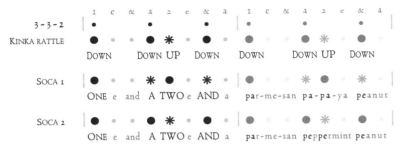

ABOVE: Adding beat 2 (the backbeat) to 3-3-2 reinforces the underlying PULSE in numerous dance styles, from 19th-century Cuban HABANERA (facing page) to traditional Ghanaian KINKA and contemporary Trinidadian SOCA (above). In soca pattern 1, the kick drum plays the beat and snare adds the remaining two notes of 3-3-2. In soca pattern 2, the kick plays 3-3-2 and snare adds the backbeat—like the down and up strokes of the kinka rattle.

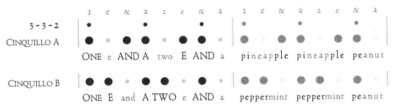

ABOVE: Adding two extra notes to the 3-3-2 rhythm produces the stick patterns of Latin American CINQUILLO, found throughout African-influenced music of the Caribbean.

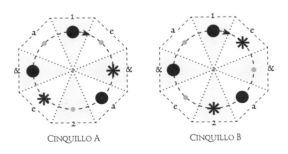

CINQUILLO A   CINQUILLO B

LEFT: In these wheel diagrams of the two Cinquillo rhythms, notice how the two additional notes are rotated, from BEFORE the original notes, in version A, to AFTER them in version B.

Reggaetón & Bhangra
the 3-3-2 continuum

The 3-3-2 pattern continues to be shared globally. In one of the Caribbean's dance crazes, REGGAETÓN, you'll hear the bass drum playing the beats, while other instruments take the second two notes of 3-3-2. These instruments might be a snare drum (as in Shabba Ranks' 1991 *Dem Bow*), keyboard, guitar, or a synthesized or sampled sound (Daddy Yankee's 2004 *Gasolina*, *opposite top*).

Many BHANGRA songs use funk and rock beats, but quite a few are propelled by 3-3-2. Qaran's *Tareefan* has 3-3-2 on both bass and bass drum (*below*). Songs like Yo Yo Honey Singh's *Gur Nalo Ishq Mitha* use the same habanera (*p.18*) combination as reggaetón's *Dem Bow*. Since bhangra draws from funk and rock, you might wonder if it also picked up 3-3-2 from there. But 3-3-2 was already a strong part of traditional Indian music, as in the cinquillo-like rhythm BHAJANI (*opposite*).

All of the above variations add notes to 3-3-2, but you can also take notes away. In the Brazilian folk/popular style BAIÃO, a bass drum plays just the first two notes of the pattern (*lower, opposite*). For an example of baião, listen to Luis Gonzaga's *Asa Branca*. But you don't have to go to Brazil to hear this variation; the horns play it on James Brown's *Super Bad*. No matter how you twist it, at least one note of 3–3–2 will be on a suspended *e* or *a*. That's one reason this rhythm is so powerful.

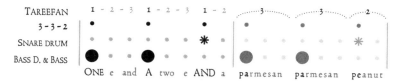

ABOVE: The REGGAETÓN rhythm is identical to the Habanera variation of 3-3-2 (pages 18–19). Here a bass drum plays the beats and a second instrument the other two notes.

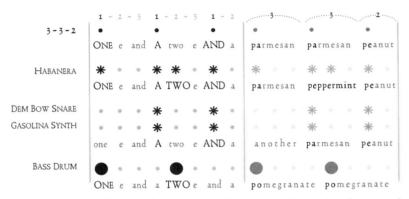

ABOVE: Rhythmic patterns for DEM BOW and GASOLINA, showing how the snare and synth play the second two notes of 3-3-2 (i.e. those which do not fall on a beat).

ABOVE: The cinquillo-like Indian rhythm BHAJANI, showing the bols used to learn it.

ABOVE: The Brazilian style Baião uses the first two notes of 3-3-2, and omits the final one.

Building with 3-3-2
call and response

Since 3-3-2 lasts just two beats, it is often paired with a contrasting rhythm for another two beats, making a four-beat pattern with a 3-3-2 half and a "straight" half, with an inherent feel of tension and release, or in African music CALL AND RESPONSE (*see idealised model, opposite top*).

Cuban SON CLAVE (*opposite*) takes its name from SON, the ancestor of MAMBO, SALSA and other related genres. In one version of son clave, the first half is the highly suspended 3-3-2, the second half is more grounded, landing firmly on beat 4 (*opposite top*). However, in many songs the two halves are switched, with the "straight" side first (*below*). Latin American musicians call the first version "3-2 CLAVE" meaning there are three notes in the first half, two in the second, and the second version "2-3 CLAVE". 3-2 may be more familiar to non-Latin audiences, but styles like salsa and mambo prefer 2-3. This is because 2-3 clave ends with suspension, propelling dancers forward into the next cycle.

KONPA, a popular dance from Haiti, uses the first two notes of 3-3-2 in its first half, then grounds firmly on both beats 3 and 4. HIGHLIFE, from Ghana and Nigeria, is elegantly suspended on *and*s all the way through its second half. KACHACHA, played in Angolan folk guitar music, includes a cinquillo (*p.16*) in the first half, followed by all four 8th notes. CASCARÁ, heard in Cuban folk and popular styles, fleshes out its clave base (the larger dots) with additional notes.

	FIRST HALF (grounded 2-2-2-2)	SECOND HALF (suspended 3-3-2)
MODEL 2 2 2 2 | 3 3 2	● · ● · ● · ● ·	● · · ● · · ● ·
2-3 SON CLAVE	· · ✶ · ✶ · · ·	✶ · · ✶ · · ✶ ·
	one e AND a TWO e and a	THREE e and A four e AND a
	and a peanut peanut and a	parmesan parmesan peanut

FIRST HALF (suspended 3-3-2)   SECOND HALF (grounded 2-2-2-2)

MODEL 3 3 2 | 2 2 2 2	● · · ● · · ● · ● · ● · ● · ● · ONE e and A two e AND a THREE e AND a FOUR e AND a parmesan parmesan peanut pitter patter pitter patter
3-2 SON CLAVE	✱ · · ✱ · · ✱ · · ✱ · ✱ · · ONE e and A two e AND a three e AND a FOUR e and a parmesan parmesan peanut and a pitter patter and a
KONPA	✱ · · ✱ · · · · ✱ · ✱ · ✱ · · ONE e and A two e and a THREE e AND a FOUR e AND a parmesan parmesan and a pitter patter putter and a
HIGHLIFE	✱ · · ✱ · · ✱ · · ✱ · · · ✱ · ONE e and A two e AND a three e AND a four e AND a parmesan parmesan peanut and a pitter and a patter
KPAACHA 3 2 3 | 2 2 2 2	✱ · · ✱ · ✱ · · ✱ · ✱ · ✱ · ONE e and A two E and a THREE e AND a FOUR e AND a parmesan peanut parmesan pitter patter pitter patter
KACHACHA	✱ ✱ · ✱ · ✱ ✱ · ✱ · ✱ · ✱ · ONE E and A two E AND a THREE e AND a FOUR e AND a peppermint peanut peppermint pitter patter pitter patter
CASCARÁ	✱ · ✱ ✱ · ✱ · ✱ ✱ · ✱ · ✱ ✱ · ✱ ONE e AND A two E and A THREE e AND a FOUR E and A peanut peppermint peanut peppermint peanut peppermint pie
SAMBA 3 3 2 | 2 3 3	✱ · · ✱ · · ✱ · · · ✱ · ✱ · · ONE e and A two e AND a three e AND a four E and a parmesan parmesan peanut and more parmesan parmesan

ABOVE: *Variations on* 3-3-2 | 2-2-2-2, *including* 3-2 SON CLAVE. FACING PAGE: *The more common reversed pattern* 2-3 SON CLAVE. NOTE: *Latin musicians count and write clave with 8th notes* (| 1 & 2 & 3 & 4 & | 1 & 2 & 3 & 4 & |) *rather than 16ths. However, we have introduced* 3-3-2 *with 16th notes* (Es *and* As), *and continue that model for consistency.*

GUIDE PATTERNS
rhythmic frames

The lively syncopations of African and Caribbean music are not just a bunch of notes off the beat, thrown together. Instead, GUIDE PATTERNS—vivid, asymmetrical patterns like 3-3-2 (*p.14*) and cinquillo (*p.16*)—tie the ensemble together, providing a rhythmic frame around which the music is built. Ethnomusicologists call these patterns TIME LINES. Latin American musicians often use the Cuban term CLAVE.

Look how the melody of a well-known mambo, Beny Moré's *Que Bueno Baile Usted*, follows 2-3 son clave (*opposite top*). The natural accents of the words match the notes of clave. Percussion instruments follow and reinforce the guide, forming the rhythms typically played in a mambo band. The large bell elaborates on clave, adding more down-up notes on the grounded 2 side and more suspended notes on the 3 side. The timbales elaborate clave with cascará. The conga leads with a slap ⊙ on the first note of clave, and has a low tone on the crucial *a* on the 3 side. Its high tones, at the end of each half, are offbeat lifts for the dancers. The offbeat is doubled to *and a* in the first half, but there is just one tone at the end, to reinforce the last note of the guide.

A beautiful and powerful ternary guide is the 12/8 pattern (*shown opposite*), found in both West and Central African traditions as well as Black cultures in the New World. In fact, this rhythm is so widespread that ethnomusicologists refer to it as "the standard pattern" or, because it is often played on an iron bell, THE STANDARD BELL. Like other guides, it is asymmetric, which helps musicians keep track of where they are in relation to it, and it organizes melodies. In this traditional Cuban song, almost every syllable matches one of the bell's notes.

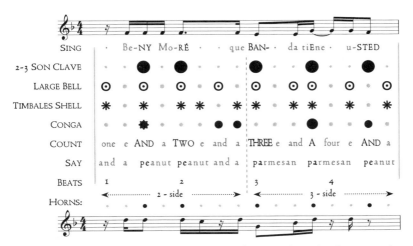

ABOVE: An example of 2-3 son clave. Beny Moré's *Que Baile Usted*, Cuba, 1940s. The conga pattern is built of a slap ✱, high tones ● and low tones ●. "Tiene" has three syllables, with the accent in the middle. All the notes of clave, except the last, are played by the horns.

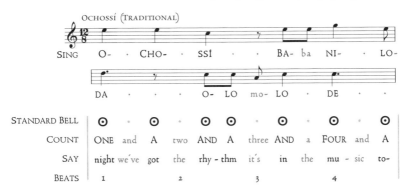

ABOVE: In this traditional Cuban song, one of many which call on the Yoruba deity OCHOSSÍ ("the hunter"), the melody matches the guide pattern on almost every syllable. The underlying beats organise the cycle into four triplets, and these are where dancers step.

OFFSET RHYTHMS & GAMELAN
turning things around

We have already seen offset rhythms in play with 3-3-2, which also twists into 3-2-3 and 2-3-3 (*see page 15*). The "standard bell" guide pattern of African and Diasporic music is another good example, as several turns of its wheel show up in various traditions (*see opposite*). Wheel A is the most common pattern, starting with the large dot at the top. Wheel B is heard frequently in Central African music and in Diasporic styles with Congolese origins, mainly from Haiti and Brazil. Other interesting turns of the wheel are illustrated.

Offsets are also used in the binary rhythms of Indonesian GAMELAN, or tuned metal percussion orchestras. A middle-sized gong, KEMPLI, marks a medium tempo "beat", to which middle-sized keys play the main melody. Lower gongs play two or four times more slowly, with the largest marking the end of a rhythmic cycle of 8, 16, or more beats. Smaller keys elaborate the melody twice as fast, and even smaller keys double or quadruple that rate. The smallest and largest instruments might be in a ratio of 64:1 (see *below*). To play the fastest parts, two musicians sit across from one another at the same instrument, playing offset interlocking patterns called KOTEKAN (*lower, opposite*).

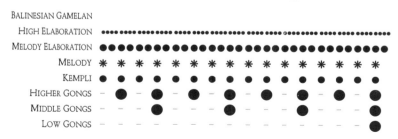

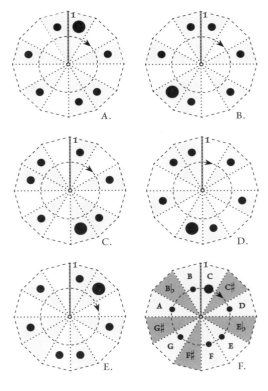

LEFT: STANDARD BELL wheels. Wheel A is the most common. Wheel B is heard in Central African and Diasporic styles and was adopted by American jazz drummers such as Art Blakey in the 1950s, as they sought to evoke African roots. Like A, B begins on the 2nd note of a double stroke. Wheel C accompanies some types of Nigerian Yoruban drumming, such as DUNDUN talking drums. Wheel D begins on a rest, but is simply A started in the middle, just like the two versions of son clave. Wheel E begins with a double stroke; we have no examples but it has a solid feel and you can experiment with it. Wheel F shows how the standard bell pattern has the same intervallic structure as the Western major scale. Turns of the wheel generate other modes. Wheel B, for example is the rhythmic equivalent of the Lydian mode.

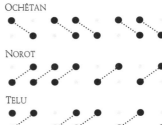

LEFT: In Balinesian gamelan, the metal keys resonate, so to prevent a cacophany, as musicians strike a key with a mallet in one hand they grab the note they previously played with the other hand, stopping its sound. Since they are playing one-handed, they achieve the rapid-fire high notes using offset KOTEKAN interlocking patterns. Two musicians play at the same time, their kotekan combinations sounding like one very fast melody.

SWING & JAZZ
the sound of modernity

In the early 20th century, musicians began to SWING, to pull notes towards a ternary feel, a subdivision by three. There are degrees of swing—you can make the ternary feel more or less obvious—but when all is said and swung, swing is ternary. This is easy to see in the SHUFFLE rhythm of blues (*opposite top*). Remove one note from every other shuffle, and you have the "spang-a-lang" JAZZ RIDE, played on a cymbal. Horn players, pianists and singers get the swing feel across by playing notes just before the beat, even though, for ease of reading, songs are written STRAIGHT (binary, *opposite centre*).

Reggae (*p.28*) is often swung. Sometimes the characteristic reggae rhythms—skank, double chop, bubble—are played straight, and sometimes swung. In Bob Marley's *Natural Mystic* everything swings to the max, even the percussion.

Jazz compositions are full of rhythmic imagination. Even a gently swinging, medium-tempo song like Duke Ellington and Billy Strayhorn's *Satin Doll* uses a few tricks (*opposite*). Lines 1 and 2 include surprising delays that arrive after downbeats (WHICH, SHE), and this effect is doubled in line 3 (OUT, MY). In addition to the ternary feel of swing, jazz musicians sometimes extend measures from the usual 2, 3, or 4 beats to 5 or even 7. An early (and surprising) hit in this vein was Dave Brubeck's 1959 *Take Five* (*below, an example of an* ODD METER, *see page 42*).

TAKE FIVE, DAVE BRUBECK

5/4	1	&	2	&	3	&	4	&	5	&
	●	✱	∘	●	✱	∘	●	∘	✱	∘
	pe	- pper	a	pe	- pper	a	pi	- nea	- pple	a

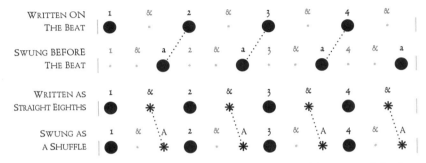

ABOVE: Ternary rhythms in blues and jazz. The SHUFFLE defines the ternary feel by playing a note before each beat. The JAZZ RIDE removes a note from every other shuffle.

ABOVE: Songs written as binary can be swung as they are played, giving a ternary feel to the rhythm. The exact amount of displacement varies, creating many swing feels.

	1	&	A	2	&	a	3	&	A	4	&	a	1	&	A	2	&	a	3	&	A	4	&	a
i.		Ci	- ga	- rette			hol	- der							WHICH				wigs		me			
ii.		O	- ver	her			shoul	- der							SHE				digs		me			
iii.			OUT				cat	- tin'							MY				sa	-	- tin		doll	
iv.	1	&	A	2	&	A	3	&	A	4	&	a	1	&	A	2	&	A	3	&	a	4	&	A
(She's) NO	-	-	bo	dy's		FOOL			so	I'm	PLAY	-	-	in'		it		COOL			as	can		BE

ABOVE: In their 1953 song *Satin Doll*, Ellington and Strayhorn's verses have surprising delays in the middle (i. & ii.), and finish by doubling this riff (iii). In the bridge (the middle part of the song), instead of delaying notes, the composers stress heavily swinging **a**s before beats.

FUNK
straightening up and getting down

By the mid 1940s, the big bands of the swing era proved too expensive to maintain. Black popular music turned to small rhythm 'n' blues ensembles of just five or six musicians (e.g. Louis Jordan and his Tympany Five). They played bluesy shuffles and jazzy swing, and started adding a strong backbeat on beats 2 and 4 with a snare drum or handclaps (e.g. Wynonie Harris' 1947 *Good Rockin' Tonight, below*).

By the mid-1960s straight rhythms (with little or no swing) dominated American popular music, in soul and, especially, FUNK. Many funk drumbeats are basically backbeats on 2 and 4 on the snare drum, with variations on 3-2 son clave in the bass/kick drum (*opposite top*). But drums are not the only element in a funk groove. All of the instruments are involved! Take a look at James Brown's 1968 *Say It Loud (I'm Black and I'm Proud)*. The drummer marks steady beats on cymbal, backbeats on snare. His kick drum suggests a stripped-down son clave, just two notes out of clave's five. The bass plays 3-3-2 in half time, a spacious but energizing feel. The rhythm guitar adds notes on beats 2 and 3. We now have a solid framework of beats, backbeats, 3-3-2, and clave (*opposite*).

WYNONIE HARRIS' *Good Rockin' Tonight*, 1947

SHUFFLE	1	&	A	2	&	A	3	&	A	4	&	A
BASS DRUM OR CYMBAL	●	·	●	●	·	●	●	·	●	●	·	●
	pi	- neap	- ple	pi	- neap	- ple	pi	- neap	- ple	pi	- neap	- ple

BACKBEAT	1	&	a	2	&	a	3	&	a	4	&	a
SNARE OR HANDCLAPS	·	·	·	✻	·	·	·	·	·	✻	·	·
	get	me	some	**par**	- me	- san	find	me	some	**par**	- me	- san

ABOVE: Typical FUNK beat, with snares on backbeats 2 and 4 and the kick drum largely following 3-2 clave, but also playing endless variations on this feel, as in the bottom line.

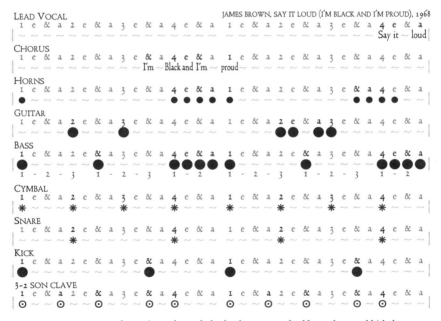

ABOVE: James Brown's *Say it Loud*. Cymbals play beats, snare backbeats, bass and kick drum suggest 3-3-2 and 3-2 clave. On top of this framework, the vocalists, guitar and horns set up an intricate call and response sequence, following and overlapping one another.

Motown, Rock, & Punk
snares on the backbeat

With the invention of the electric guitar, Black musicians like Chuck Berry put rhythm n' blues on steroids. White musicians soon copied them, and rock n' roll was born. Early rock hits like Chuck Berry's 1958 *Johnny B. Goode* and Elvis Presley's 1956 *Hound Dog* were shuffles with backbeats, but increasing numbers of popular songs soon abandoned swing (ternary) for straight (binary) rhythms.

Rock drummers simplified funk's clave-influenced structure, dropping the suspended *e*s and *a*s in favor of beats and offbeat ***and***s (*below*). Though there are no *e*s or *a*s in the rock pattern, it still retains a clave-like call and response: beats 1 and 2 answered by beats 3 and 4 (*opposite*).

The overall rhythmic feel of much rock seems denser than funk, chiefly due to distortion and reverb on the guitars, and to drummers playing on large cymbals that ring on and on. When punk blasted into public consciousness, one of its defining features was its speed and constant run of notes, which evoked anger and alarm instead of the pleasureable dance-friendly tempos of funk, rock and disco.

	1	e	&	a	2	e	&	a	3	e	&	a	4	e	&	a
3-2 SON CLAVE	◉			◉			◉				◉		◉			
FUNK SNARE					✱								✱			
FUNK KICK	●			●			●		●		●					
ROCK SNARE					✱								✱			
ROCK KICK	●								●		●					

| ● · * · | ● ● * · |1. | ● · * · | ● ● * ● |2.
|---|---|
| ONE & TWO & THREE AND FOUR & | ONE & TWO AND THREE AND FOUR AND |
| pu - sh cha - nk pe - pper cha - nk | pu - sh cha - nk pe - pper cho - pper |

ABOVE: 1. This BASIC BEAT, with its backbeat snare and call-and-response, is the foundation of MOTWN hits such as: Jr. Walker & The All Stars *Shotgun*; Wilson Pickett *In the Midnight Hour*. It also appears in many ROCK hits: Jimi Hendrix *Purple Haze*; The Rolling Stones *Brown Sugar*. 2. The COMMON VARIATION, heard in: Stevie Wonder *Fingertips*; The Beatles *Ticket to Ride*.

| ● · * ● | ● · * · |3. | ● · * ● | ● · * · |4.
|---|---|
| ONE & TWO AND THREE & FOUR & | ONE & TWO AND 3 AND FOUR & |
| pu - sh cho - pper pu - sh cha - nk | pull a cho - pper or por - chi - ni |

| ● · * · | ● · * · |5. | ● ● * · | ● ● * · |6.
|---|---|
| ONE & TWO & THREE & FOUR & | ONE AND TWO & THREE AND FOUR & |
| pu - sh cha - nk pu - sh cha - nk | pe - pper cha - nk pe - pper cha - nk |

ABOVE: FUTHER VARIATIONS on the basic beat: 3. The Temptations *Ain't Too Proud to Beg*; Blondie *Shayla* 4. Smokey Robinson & The Miracles *Tracks of my Tears*. 5. The call half as the whole pattern: AC/DC *Highway to Hell* (chorus). 6. The response half as the whole pattern: Nirvana *Smells Like Teen Spirit*. NOTE: All six examples are often mixed into longer patterns.

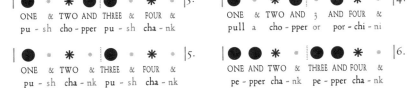

SUBDIVIDED I — ONE e & a TWO e & A THREE e AND a FOUR e & a |7.
SUBDIVIDED II — ONE e & a TWO e & A 3 E AND a FOUR e & a |8.

ABOVE: Adding "a"s and "e"s to the basic beat can put an extra kick in the rhythm: 7. Aerosmith *Walk This Way*. 8. Guns n' Roses, *Don't Cry*; The Eagles *Hotel California*. Iconic guitar riffs often begin grounded on beat 1 or 2, moving to offbeat "&"s for excitement, returning to the beat at the end.

PUNK SNARE
KICK & BASS
ONE AND TWO AND THREE AND FOUR AND pe - pper pe - pper pe - pper pe - pper

ABOVE: On classic punk songs like the Sex Pistols' *Anarchy in the UK* and The Ramones *Teenage Lobotomy*, both the kick drum and bass play a nearly constant run of eighth notes, "**beat and**". There is no pausing for breath, no room for debate, no escaping the intensity.

HIP-HOP, D&B, & TRAP
exercises in tempo

Since, the 1980s, funk grooves have been extended in many ways, particularly in the world of electronic music, where many genres rely on technology to carefully control the tempo.

HIP-HOP beats have a relatively slow tempo, around 90*bpm* (beats per minute). They are mostly played straight (binary), but their slow speed occasionally allows room for a subtle swing feel, using triplets and even sextuplets (six subdivisions per beat). You can hear this in De La Soul's *Stakes is High*. The BOOM BAP subgenre of hip-hop also specialises in slightly swung "lazy beats", e.g. in A Tribe Called Quest's *Electric Relaxation*. TRIP HOP is another subgenre that slows the tempo, but adds fewer fast subdivisions and creates a more relaxed feel. TRAP is played between 120–160*bpm*, but often has a half-time feel, so can be perceived as a very slow 60–80*bpm* (the use of double-time hi-hats and snare rolls also make the music feel faster).

DRUM & BASS takes the opposite tack, speeding up the underlying beats to around 180bpm, often even faster than punk (*see p.30*). Drum & bass uses basic rock and funk beats, but at a tempo where they virtually become a flow, dense and energetic. The heavy bottom combines with sustained, floating synth melodies and psychedelic effects for this style's distinctive sound. A related genre, JUNGLE, at around 170*bpm*, combines D&B with reggae: fast notes on higher instruments, slower notes on kick drum and bass. In Code Red's *Conquering Lion*, the high-hat plays a fast D&B rhythm, while the kick plays a stretched-out 3-3-2. At 140*bpm* DUBSTEP, characterised by its wobbly bass sound and higher levels of subdivisions is slower still.

DRUM & BASS *basic*
● · · · ✱ · · · | · · ● · ✱ · · · | 1.
ONE e & a TWO e & a 3 e AND a FOUR e and a
pick a chi - lli or por - chi - ni

TRIP HOP
● · ● · ✱ · · · | · · ●● ✱ · · · | 2.
ONE e AND a TWO e and a three e AND A FOUR e and a
pea - nut pea - nut chi - lli and a love - ly pe - pper chi - lli and a

AMEN BREAK
· · ● · ✱ · · ✱ | · ✱ ● ● ✱ · · ✱ | 3.
ONE e AND a TWO e and A three E AND A FOUR e it A
pea - nut pea - nut chi - lli it - chy it - chy pe - pper chi - lli it - chy

ABOVE: 1. The DRUM & BASS model uses the basic rock beat (p.31), but removes its kick on beat 3, and increases the tempo up to 180bpm, as in Netsky's Eyes Closed. 2. In the more relaxed rhythms of TRIP HOP, the structure is often the same, but the bpm is around 100bpm, allowing room for extra kicks, hear Rob Dougan's Clubbed to Death. 3. The famous 136bpm AMEN BREAK has the same kick structure, but throws in some additional "e"s and "a"s.

HIP-HOP *example*
● · · · ✱ · ●● | · ●● · ✱ · · ✱ | 4.
ONE e & a TWO e AND A 3 E AND a FOUR e & A
pea - nut and a chi - lli pe - pper a pe - pper - mint chi - lli a cheap

If I Ruled the World
● · ◉ · ✱ · ◉ · | · ●◉● ✱ · ◉ · | 5.
ONE e AND a TWO e AND A 3 E AND a FOUR e AND a
pea - nut dish a chi - lli di - pper a - pple di - pping chi - lli dish a

ABOVE: HIP-HOP slows down the tempo to around 90bpm. 5. Kurtis Blow's If I Ruled the World, an early hip-hop classic, uses cowbells on every "&", to put the "hip" in the "hop".

BOOM BAP
● · · ● ✱ · ● · | · · · ● · ✱ · · | 6.
ONE e & A TWO e AND a 3 e AND a FOUR e & a
par - me - san pat - chou - li pea - nut and a pea - nut chi - lli and a

TRAP *example*
● · · · ✱ · ● · | · · ● · ✱ · ✱✱✱ | 7.
ONE e & a TWO e AND a three e AND a FOUR e & a
po - me - gra - nate chi - lli pea - nut it's a pea - nut chi - lli dz zz zz

ABOVE: BOOM BAP is played around 90bpm, TRAP around 140bpm. These two examples are both related to 3-2 son clave: 6. Geto Boys' Mind Playing Tricks on Me; Enigma Sadeness.

Polyrhythm
one, two, three, hemiola

Play two or more contrasting rhythms at the same time, and you create POLYRHYTHM. One pattern sets the scene, the others are CROSS-RHYTHMS. The most basic polyrhythm contrasts the two most common musical numbers, 2 and 3 (*opposite top*). This combination is known as 3-AGAINST-2, a crossrhythm of three notes against a foundation of two notes (which are also the beats). It works because there are six subdivisions, and six can be divided evenly by both two and three.

3-against-2 played twice creates 6-AGAINST-4. This happens naturally when the music is in a four-beat rather than a two-beat cycle. Twelve subdivsions also enables you to play 3-AGAINST-4 (*opposite centre*).

Instead of playing 3 and 2 at the same time as a polyrhythm, you can play 3-FOLLOWED-BY-2. This is HEMIOLA, as is 2-FOLLOWED-BY-3 (*see example from West Side Story below*). Latin American styles such as Venezuelan JOROPO, Mexican SON JAROCHO and Colombian PASILLO combine the feels of both 3-3-2 and hemiola, with stringed instruments playing both feels.

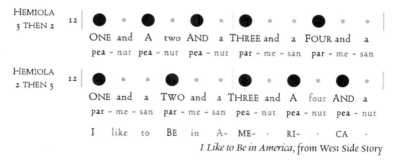

I Like to Be in America, from West Side Story

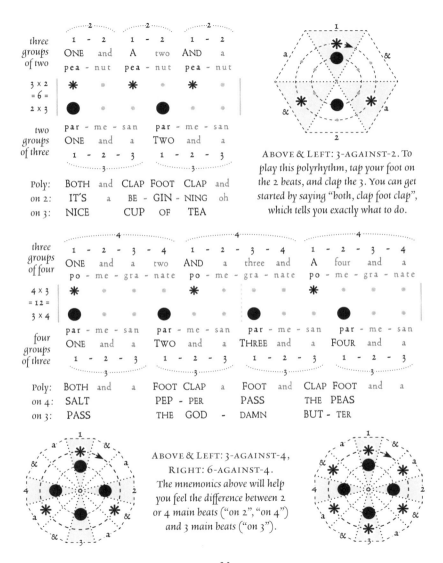

	⌒2	⌒2	⌒2
three groups of two	1 - 2 ONE and pea - nut	1 - 2 A two pea - nut	1 - 2 AND a pea - nut
3 × 2 = 6 = 2 × 3	✱ ✱ ● ● ● ●	✱ ● ● ● ● ●	✱ ✱ ● ● ● ●
two groups of three	par - me - san ONE and a 1 - 2 - 3 ⌣3		par - me - san TWO and a 1 - 2 - 3 ⌣3
Poly: on 2: on 3:	BOTH and IT'S a NICE	CLAP FOOT BE - GIN - CUP OF	CLAP and NING oh TEA

ABOVE & LEFT: 3-AGAINST-2. To play this polyrhythm, tap your foot on the 2 beats, and clap the 3. You can get started by saying "both, clap foot clap", which tells you exactly what to do.

	⌒4	⌒4	⌒4
three groups of four	1 - 2 - 3 - 4 ONE and a two	1 - 2 - 3 - 4 AND a three and	1 - 2 - 3 - 4 A four and a
	po - me - gra - nate	po - me - gra - nate	po - me - gra - nate
4 × 3 = 12 = 3 × 4	✱ ● ● ● ● ● ● ●	✱ ● ● ● ● ● ● ●	✱ ● ● ● ● ● ● ●
four groups of three	par - me - san ONE and a 1 - 2 - 3	par - me - san TWO and a 1 - 2 - 3	par - me - san THREE and a 1 - 2 - 3
Poly: on 4: on 3:	BOTH and a SALT PASS	FOOT CLAP a PEP - PER THE GOD -	FOOT and PASS DAMN

(continued: CLAP FOOT and a / THE PEAS / BUT - TER; FOUR and a)

ABOVE & LEFT: 3-AGAINST-4, RIGHT: 6-AGAINST-4. The mnemonics above will help you feel the difference between 2 or 4 main beats ("on 2", "on 4") and 3 main beats ("on 3").

More Polyrhythm
bembe and agbekor

World traditions present endlessly fascinating, creative instances of polyrhythms. The basic numbers 2 and 3 are at the bottom of most of them. You will also find complex combinations based on other numbers (5, 7 and so forth) in contemporary Western "art" composition and jazz, and in the highly sophisticated world of South Asian music, but 2 and 3 give rise to complexity all on their own.

In the simplified rendition of Afrocuban BEMBE shown opposite, a shaker ✷ marks the four main beats, reinforced by a high drum playing each beat and second subdivision, **beat and** (dancers also step mainly on these beats). The middle drum plays on 2 and 3 (doubled), 5 and 6 (also doubled); this suggests a feel of 6. With these three instruments, then, we have the polyrhythm 6-against-4 (*opposite top*). The bell ☉ plays the asymmetrical "standard pattern", reinforced by the low drum. Finally, the sticks create an illusory 3-against-4 (the real main beats are played by the shaker).

The Ewe people of Ghana often play in large percussion ensembles with a lead drum, three or even four support drums, bells and shakers. The lead drum plays compositions based on spoken language and changes constantly, but the other instruments usually play repeating patterns. In the Ewe dance AGBEKOR, shakers mark the four beats underlying the standard bell. The high drum plays the offbeat subdivisions of each beat. The middle drum divides the measure in half, with notes leading to beats 2 and 4. The lowest drum plays 3-2 hemiola (*see p.34*). It also reinforces the bell, matching the bell on four of its five notes.

Beats (4)	1	&	a	2	&	a	3	&	a	4	&	a
Shaker	✱	·	·	✱	·	·	✱	·	·	✱	·	·
High Drum	●	●	·	●	●	·	●	●	·	●	●	·

Beats (6)	1	&	2	&	3	&	4	&	5	&	6	&
Middle Drum	·	·	●	·	●	●	·	·	●	·	●	●
Bell	◉	·	◉	·	◉	◉	·	◉	·	◉	·	◉
Low Drum	●	·	·	·	·	·	·	·	·	·	·	·
Variation	●	·	·	·	·	●	●	·	●	·	●

Quasi-Beats (3)	1	e	&	a	2	e	&	a	3	e	&	a
Sticks	✱	·	✱	✱	✱	·	✱	✱	✱	·	✱	✱

ABOVE: AFROCUBAN BEMBE. *The shaker and high drum mark the four beats, the middle drum marks the six. The bell plays the asymmetric "standard pattern". The low drum's basic part is simply the downbeat, but it plays innumerable variations, mostly based on the of the bell. The clashing crossrhythms of the ensemble, together with songs and the collective belief of the community, create an intense spiritual experience.*

Beats (4)	1	&	a	2	&	a	3	&	a	4	&	a
Shaker	✱	·	·	✱	·	·	✱	·	·	✱	·	·
High Drum	·	●	●	·	●	·	·	●	●	·	●	●
Middle Drum	·	●	●	●	·	·	·	●	●	●	·	·
Bell	◉	·	◉	·	◉	◉	·	◉	·	◉	·	◉
Low Drum	●	·	●	·	●	·	●	·	·	●	·	·
	1	&	2	&	3	&	1	&	a	2	&	a

ABOVE: GHANAIAN AGBEKOR. *Shakers, spaced by two taps on a high drum, mark the four beats underlying the standard bell. The low drum plays hemiola. Against this steady framework, a lead drum plays intricate language-based compositions, while dancers both follow the lead drum's phrases and depict scenes from Ewe history.*

Further Polyrhythm
kadodo and flamenco

KADODO, another Ewe dance, features an elaborate polyrhythm. Its guide pattern spans a full twenty-four subdivisions (*below*). The bell starts the dance on its own, before the other instruments join, and you're likely to hear it as playing a cinquillo-like pattern in two-beat measures (*illusory beats*). But the actual feel is eight triplets. This becomes evident when the rest of the ensemble enters, as dancers step on these real main beats, while supporting drums divide the cycle into four groups of six subdivisions each. Rattles also mark the main beats, but, as if the polyrhythm isn't already complex enough, they subdivide each beat binarily into two: **8-AGAINST-12**.

Handclapping, or *palmas*, is an essential part of **FLAMENCO**, and is often polyrhythmic. One person claps a basic pattern (with variations), another claps offbeats (**CONTRATIEMPO**). Many flamenco rhythms have a count of twelve notes. All twelve are clapped, but some are accented. Those clapping the basic part cup their palms for a low sound; those clapping the crossrhythms slap fingers on palms for a high sound. Examples of **BULERIAS**, **TANGO** and **ONE OTHER** are shown opposite.

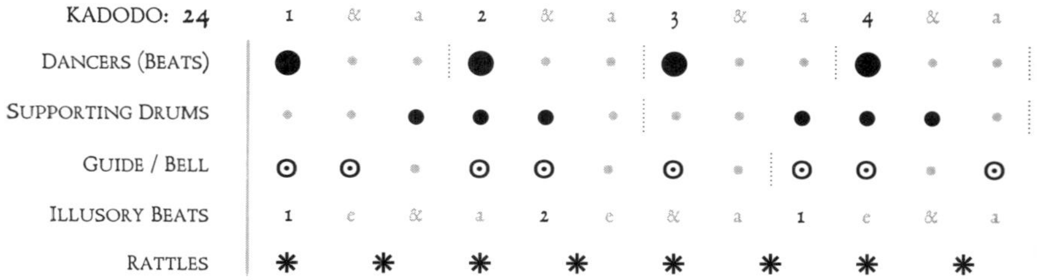

KADODO: 24	1	&	a	2	&	a	3	&	a	4	&	a
DANCERS (BEATS)	●	·	·	●	·	·	●	·	·	●	·	·
SUPPORTING DRUMS	·	·	●	●	●	·	·	·	●	●	●	·
GUIDE / BELL	⊙	⊙	·	⊙	⊙	·	⊙	·	⊙	⊙	·	⊙
ILLUSORY BEATS	1	e	&	a	2	e	&	a	1	e	&	a
RATTLES	✱		✱		✱		✱		✱	✱		✱

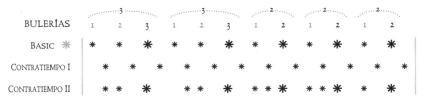

ABOVE: The basic pattern of the 12-note FLAMENCO rhythm BULERÍAS is a hemiola (see page 34). The last note in each group is accented, and clapping usually begins on the final note of the cycle. CONTRATIEMPO clapping can slide in between each of the main notes (I), or create a more elaborate pattern that nonetheless keeps the shape of the main rhythm (II).

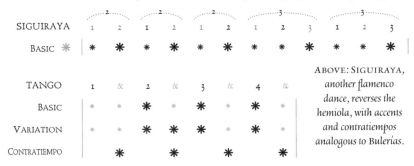

ABOVE: SIGUIRAYA, another flamenco dance, reverses the hemiola, with accents and contratiempos analogous to Bulerías.

ABOVE: A few flamenco rhythms have a count of four notes. TANGOS omit the downbeat. These combinations may only have two parts, but make no mistake: the tempos can be quite fast and the clapping loud; they are intense. BELOW: The Ewe KADODO dance has a highly sophisticated guide pattern of 24 subdivisions, yet is all based on 2 and 3.

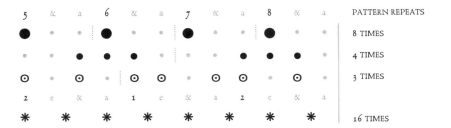

Polymeter
and metric modulation

POLYMETER is polyrhythm on steroids: contrasting patterns in different feels. In the Cuban dance RUMBA COLOMBIA, as played in the town of Puerto Cardenas, two groups of instruments share a cycle of four main beats, but subdivide those beats differently: one group subdivides by three and the other by four. It's 4/4 against 12/8 (*opposite top*).

METRIC MODULATION moves from one meter to another, modifying beats, subdivisions and measures alike. In his improvised solos, the great Cuban conga player Mongo Santamaria sometimes began a 3-against-2 polyrhythmic riff, before introducing a sequence of four notes on the congas, Mid-High-Mid-Low, sounding like a new four-beat measure (*below*). In improvised solos like this, musicians mostly soon return to the basic groove. Contemporary composers, however, sometimes let the new feel dominate for extended periods, or keep it superimposed over the original to create multilayered polymetric webs.

These examples still only work with the numbers 2 and 3. Musicians in India's Hindustani and Carnatic traditions, art music composers, prog-rockers like Frank Zappa, and jazz musicians like Steve Coleman may add fives, sevens, or other numbers to the mix (*e.g. center opposite*).

QUAD COUNT	1	e	&	a	2	e	&	a	1	e	&	a	2	e	&	a
BEAT	●	·	·	·	●	·	·	·	●	·	·	·	●	·	·	·
3-vs-2 COUNT (6)	1		&		2		&		3		&		1		&		2		&		3		&
3-vs-2 BEAT	●	·	●	·	●	·	●	·	●	·	●	·
3-vs-2 COUNT (8)	1		&		2		&		3		&		4		&		1		&		2		&
CONGA: MID, HI, LOW	**M**	·	**H**	·	**M**	·	**L**	·	**M**	·	**H**	·

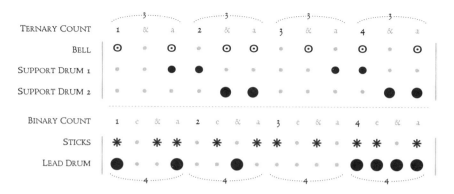

ABOVE: *One version of the Cuban dance* RUMBA COLOMBIA *divides the cycle into both 12 and 16. The lead drum improvises; this example shows it playing 3-3-2 in the first half and a fast flurry of notes towards the end.*

ABOVE: *Advanced musicians can work with numbers beyond the basic 2 and 3. Nature does all the time. This pattern occurs between the five major* ● *and five minor* • *conjuctions of the Sun and Venus over eight Earth years* ✻ *, producing an 8:10 (or 4:5) polymeter.*

BELOW: *Example of polymeter from Mongo Santamaria's Ti Mon Bo (3:18). Note how the introduction of 3-vs-2 changes the subdivisions, making them ternary; Santamaria then regroups them into new measures using the melodic pattern M-H-M-L.*

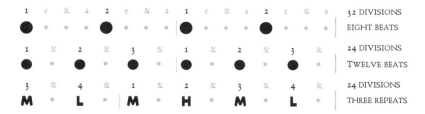

Uneven Beats & Odd Meters
around the Mediterranean

What about numbers other than 2, 3 and 4? Why shouldn't beats be subdivided by 5? Can measures be 5 beats long, or 7, or even longer?

Such numbers are in common practice in the music of Eastern Europe and the Arab world, from the Balkans and Greece through Turkey, the Levant, Iraq and Iran, Egypt, and on across North Africa. They do utilise 2 and 3, but build longer sequences. Thus, 5 can be 2-3 or 3-2, and 7 can be 2-2-3 or 3-2-2.

In this kind of rhythm, the subdivisions stay the same length, so beats with three subdivisions are longer than those with two. That's right, the beats are no longer evenly spaced. Dancers and musicians speak of these as LONG and SHORT beats. The Turkish term for such rhythms is AKSAK, "limping", but for musicians and dancers accustomed to them, they flow just as smoothly as any other kind of rhythm. Western musicians often call them ODD METER (*opposite*).

In music that uses such rhythms, they function much as guide patterns do in African and Caribbean music, organizing melodies and instrumental accompaniment. The melody of the Serbian song *Adje Jano* follows the rhythmic pattern 3-2-2 (7) (*below*).

ADJE JANO (Bulgaria), *transcription courtesy Mary Kay Brass*

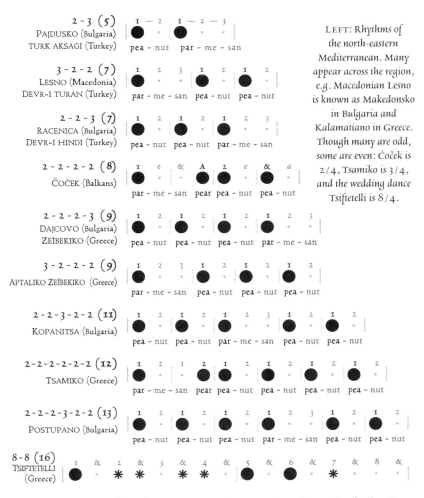

LEFT: Rhythms of the north-eastern Mediterranean. Many appear across the region, e.g. Macedonian Lesno is known as Makedonsko in Bulgaria and Kalamatiano in Greece. Though many are odd, some are even: Čoček is 2/4, Tsamiko is 3/4, and the wedding dance Tsiftetelli is 8/4.

ABOVE: Rhythms are often defined by tempo as well as pattern: the Habanera-like **ČOČEK** is driving; **LESNO** is slow and anchors many romantic songs; **TSAMIKO** (or **TSAMIKOS**) begins the same as Čoček, but is played more slowly as the basis for beautiful modal improvisations.

IQA'AT CYCLES
rhythms of the Persian and Arabic world

Arabic music uses rhythmic patterns called IQA'AT (singular IQA'). They are defined not just by time but also timbre, using drum mnemonics: a sustained bass DUM ● and a high snappy TAK ✱. For example, the first three patterns shown (*opposite top*) have identical note values, but different tones on accompanying percussion. The timbral differences gives these patterns distinct feels, and they are likely to be used in different musical styles—SAIDI in traditional dancing from Egypt's Said region; MAQSUM in popular recordings for its lively, forward motion; BALADI, with its low second note, for a more grounded feel. A single composition can switch back and forth between many different *iqa'at*. Various popular rhythms from the Arabic world are shown opposite.

Many Persian rhythms are in 6/8 time, played at various tempos on a TONBAK goblet drum and a DAF frame drum (*see examples below*).

	1	&	2	&	3	&	4	&	5	&	6	&
PERSIAN 6/4	●				✱	✱	●					
	dum				tak	tak	dum					
TONBAK 6/8	●				✱	✱	●		✱			
	dum				tak	tak	dum		tak			
RENG	●		✱	✱		●		✱				
	dum		tak	tak		dum		tak				
PERSIAN 6/8	●		✱	✱	✱		●		✱			
	dum		tak	tak	tak		dum		tak			

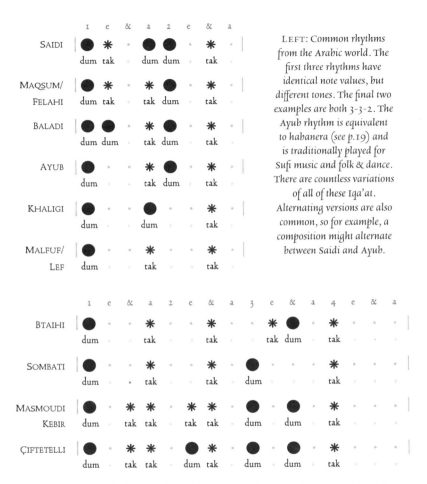

LEFT: Common rhythms from the Arabic world. The first three rhythms have identical note values, but different tones. The final two examples are both 3-3-2. The Ayub rhythm is equivalent to habanera (see p.19) and is traditionally played for Sufi music and folk & dance. There are countless variations of all of these Iqa'at. Alternating versions are also common, so for example, a composition might alternate between Saidi and Ayub.

ABOVE: Longer rhythms. The beautiful BTAIHI rhythm comes from the Tunisian Sufi tradition. MASMOUDI and ÇIFTETELLI rhythms are heard from Turkey to Egypt, and are often associated with belly dancing. All four rhythms exhibit the contrasting halves (3-3-2 and straight) typical of African and Caribbean guide patterns (see p. 22).

Middle Eastern Rhythms
classical cycles

Middle Eastern rhythms can be evenly subdivided like Maqsum or Ciftetelli (*p.45*), or use subdivisions grouped unevenly in 2s and 3s, like Balkan music. Longer patterns may be assembled from shorter ones. To take a Turkish example, the 15-beat RAKSAN rhythm is comprised of the 8-beat 3-3-2 NIM SOFYAN and the 7-beat DEVR-I HINDI (*opposite*).

There are also long, slower rhythmic cycles, heard mainly in classical styles (*opposite centre*). The melodies of these classical Arabic pieces can be long and subtle, and singers treat them flexibly, with numerous improvised ornamentations, always with *iqa'at* as their rhythmic basis. The melody of the slow fourteen-beat cycle MUHJAR is a good example. Opposite we see the opening of the muhjar *Hal ala l astar* as sung by Ghada Shbeir, with its 14 beats.

Arabic rhythms can be evenly subdivided like those above, or use subdivisions grouped unevenly in 2s and 3s, like Balkan music (*p.42*). In both slow and fast cycles, drummers ornament the skeleton of *dums* and *taks* by filling in subdivisions. This is not random: different musical styles have characteristic accompaniments, with exciting fills for dancing, and sparse punctuations for classical songs. Arabic *iqa'at* are often described as "rhythmic modes," and the idea is apt: they are entire approaches—rhythm, timbre and variations working together.

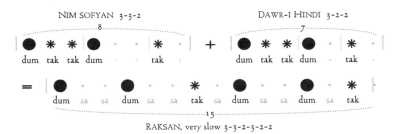

ABOVE: *Iqa'at rhythms can be combined to form longer patterns. Here the 15-beat* RAKSAN *rhythm is built from the 8-beat Nim Sofyan and the 7-beat Dawr-i Hindi.* BELOW: *Two other long rhythmic cycles, the 10-beat* SAMA' I THAQIL *and the 14-beat* MUHJAR.

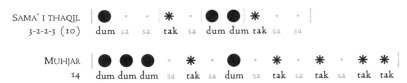

ABOVE: *"Hal ala l astar" is a slow 14-beat* MUHJAR *(one measure lasts about thirteen seconds). Long cycles like this may contain a secondary internal structure. "Hal ala" divides its fourteen beats into 8 + 6, typical for muhjar. Despite variation the internal 8 + 6 structure remains clear. Note: This rough transcription does not include the characteristic Arabic quarter-tones, nor Shbeir's inspired ornamentations around the written notes.*
FACING PAGE: ÇIFTETELLI *with characteristic fills for dancing.*

47

NORTH INDIAN RHYTHM
claps, waves, bols

Hindustani (North Indian) TAL is a rhythmic system that has been passed down orally for centuries. A TAL is a rhythmic skeleton, providing support for compositions and improvisations. Tals are sudivided into smaller units, VIBHAGAS, with claps ✻ (TALI, either clapped or struck on small cymbals) and waves ∼ (KHALI, gestured with a gentle sweep of the hand away from the body).

To fill out this skeleton, rhythmic notes are vocalized with syllables derived from the sounds of classical Hindustani drums: *na, tin, ti, ta, dha, dhin* and others (*below*). These are called BOLS. Bols are inserted into a tal to form a characteristic rhythmic pattern, known as a THEKA. Some popular examples are shown (*opposite*).

BOL	DRUM TONE & TECHNIQUE
Na/Ta/Da	Ringing tone; *played on the high drum's outer ring (chanti)*
Tin	Resonant tone; *played on the high drum's middle ring (maidan)*
Ti/Te	Dry slapping sound; *played in the high drum's black circle (syahi)*
Tu/Tun	Full resonant sound; *played near the syahi/maidan boundary*
Ga/Ge/Gi	Resonant tone; *played on the low drum's middle ring (maidan)*
Ka/Kat/Ki	Dry palm slap; *played on the low drum's syahi*
Dhin	*Ga and Tin played at the same time*
Dha/Da	*Na/Ta and Ga/Ge played at the same time*
DhaGe	*Dha and Ge played in a row*
TiRiKaTa	*Ti, Ti, Ka and Ti played quickly in a row*

DADRA TAL 6 BEATS (3 - 3, x0)

✱			~		
dha	dhin	na	dha	tin	na

TIVRA TAL 7 BEATS (3 - 2 - 2, x23)

✱			✱		✱	
dha	dhin	ta	tita	kata	gadee	gena

RUPAK TAL 7 BEATS (3 - 2 - 2, 0x2)

○			✱		✱	
tin	tin	na	dhin	na	dhin	na

KEHERWA TAL 8 BEATS (4 - 4, x0)

✱		~					
dha	ge	na	ti	na	ge	dhi	na

SUL TAL 10 BEATS (2 - 2 - 2 - 2 - 2, x0230)

✱		○	✱		~	✱		~	
dha	dha	dhin	ta	kat	dha	tite	kata	gadi	gena

JHAP TAL 10 BEATS (2 - 3 - 2 - 3, x203)

✱		✱			○		✱		
dhi	na	dhi	dhi	na	tin	na	dhi	dhi	na

EK TAL (& CHAU TAL) 12 BEATS (2 - 2 - 2 - 2 - 2 - 2, x02034)

✱		○		✱		~		✱		✱	
dhin	dhin	dhage	tirikata	tu	na	kat	ta	dhage	tirikata	dhin	na

JHOOMRA TAL 14 BEATS (3 - 4 - 3 - 4, x203)

✱			✱				~			✱			
dhin	dha	tirikata	dhin	dhin	dhage	tirikata	tin	ta	tirikata	dhin	dhin	dhage	tirikata

DIPCHANDI TAL 14 BEATS (3 - 4 - 3 - 4, x203)

✱			✱				~			✱			
dha	dhin	-	dha	dhin	-	ta	tin	-	dha	dha	dhin	-

DHAMAR TAL 14 BEATS (5 - 2 - 3 - 4, x203)

✱					✱		~			✱			
ka	dhi	te	dhi	te	dha	-	ga	ti	te	ti	te	ta	-

ADA CHAU TAL 14 BEATS (2 - 2 - 2 - 2 - 2 - 2 - 2, x203040)

✱		✱					~		✱			~	
dhin	tirikata	dhi	na	tu	na	kat	ta	dhi	dhi	na	dhi	dhi	na

TILWADA TAL 16 BEATS (4 - 4 - 4 - 4, x203)

✱				✱				~				✱			
dha	tirikata	dhin	dhin	dha	dha	tin	tin	ta	tirikata	dhin	dhin	dha	dha	dhin	dhin

TIN TAL 16 BEATS (4 - 4 - 4 - 4, x203)

✱				✱				~				✱			
dha	dhin	dhin	dha	dha	dhin	dhin	dha	dha	tin	tin	ta	ta	dhin	dhin	dha

LEFT: *Some of the most commonly used North Indian tals, arranged by length. Tals are divided into shorter subunits,* VIBHAGAS, *which are usually marked by an initial clap* ✱ (x, 1, 2, 3) *or a wave* ~ (o). *The individual beats within each rhythmic cycle are called* MATRAS, *with the first beat being called the* SAM (x). *The insertion of* BOLS *(facing page) into this framework creates the full rhythmic phrase, known as a* THEKA.

TALA VARIATIONS
composition and improvisation

Imaginative, virtuosic and mathematical rhythmic ideas play a large role in Indian music. One way musicians improvise is by taking fragments, or RHYTHMIC CELLS, from the theme and recombining them in different ways (*e.g. opposite top*). Take KAYDA, a type of short composition in the sixteen-unit cycle tin tal with three claps and a wave. A musician might use the notes highlighted, *dha ti ta* (A) and *dha dha ti ta* (B). Four A's and one B equals sixteen notes, neatly filling one half of the tala (*opposite bottom*). Notice that B is at the end of the variation: **A A A A B**. There are then four other permutations of **A** and **B**, and musicians can use any of them. Such permutations give performers an enormous vocabulary to explore.

The roots of this practice are found in the ancient Vedic tradition of reciting sacred texts containing long permutations of the names and attributes of Hindu gods and goddesses. The *khali* wave represents Kali, goddess of destruction, and she evokes emptiness by avoiding low, earthy sounds. The system therefore incorporates motion, emotion, symbolic and religious meaning right at the core of rhythm. Avid listeners often participate in performances with the gestures of the particular tala, embodying its shaping of time, its tension and release.

Compositions and improvisations almost always end with a TIHAI, a phrase played three times, ending on beat 1 of the tal cycle. This beat is called SAM (summation). The tihai creates tension against the rhythmic skeleton of the tal; its ending on sam comes as a resolution. Audiences often applaud enthusiastically when a well-executed tihai reaches its satisfying conclusion.

TIN TAL 16 BEATS (4+4+4+4, x203)

1	2	3	4	5	6	7	8	9	10	11	12	13	14	15	16
CLAP	tap	tap	tap	CLAP	tap	tap	tap	WAVE	tap	tap	tap	CLAP	tap	tap	tap
✳	·	·	·	✳	·	·	·	~	·	·	·	✳	·	·	·

STANDARD TIN TAL THEKA

dha	dhin	dhin	dha	dha	dhin	dhin	dha	dha	tin	tin	ta	ta	dhin	dhin	dha

KAYDA (composition in TIN TAL)

dha ti ta dha	ti ta	dha dha	ti ta	dha ge	tin na	kin na	ta ti	ta ta	ti ta	ta ta	ti ta	dha ge	chin na	gi na
dha ti ta		dha dha	ti ta											
{---A---}		{-----B-----}												

KAYDA IMPROVISATION

| dha ti | ta dha | ti ta | dha ti | ta dha | ti ta | dha dha | ti ta | ta ti | ta ta | ti ta | ta ta | ti ta | dha ge | chin na | gi na |
| {---A---} | {---A---} | | {---A---} | {---A---} | | {-----B-----} | | | | | | | | | |

```
A  A  A  A  B
A  A  A  B  A
A  A  B  A  A
A  B  A  A  A
B  A  A  A  A
```

ABOVE: A KAYDA compostion in tin tal, and an example of improvisation, in which two sequences of notes, A (dha ti ta) and B (dha dha ti ta), are selected from the composition and then recombined to form a new first half of the cycle (4A and 1B = 16). LEFT: There are a total of five ways of placing B within this structure. Note that in this example the original composition returns in the second half.

TIN TAL TIHAI (ending)

1	2	3	4	5	6	7	8	9	10	11	12	13	14	15	16	SAM
CLAP	tap	tap	tap	CLAP	tap	tap	tap	WAVE	tap	tap	tap	CLAP	tap	tap	tap	
✳	·	·	·	✳	·	·	·	~	·	·	·	✳	·	·	·	
ki ta	ka ta	te re	ki ta	dha	-	-	-	ki ta	ka ta	te re	ki ta	dha	-	-	-	ki ta ka ta te re ki ta dha

ABOVE: a TIHAI phrase is played three times, ending with a final downbeat SAM. If the three groupings are played with two groupings of rests, which are equally long, as above, then the tihai is called DUMDAAR. Otherwise, if there are no rests between the three groupings, then the tihai is called BEDUMDAAR (or for short, Bedum). The dumdaar above has the pattern 9-3-9-9, but a more simple one, based on the standard tin tal at the top, might be 4-2-4-2-4. In a 10-beat tal such as jhap tal (p.49) the pattern might be 6-1-6-1-6. Starting each repetition in a different place relative to the beat is known as DISPLACEMENT (see p. 55).

CARNATIC RHYTHM
the primordial echo

Despite sharing deep roots with their Northern counterparts, South India's classical Carnatic percussionists take a distinct approach to constructing their grooves. Each rhythmic cycle, or TALAM, is composed of ANGAS ('limbs') of three main types: ANUDHRUTAM (1-clap phrase), DHRUTAM (2-clap phrase), and LAGHU (variable phrase of 3/4/5/7/9 claps). Each talam calls for a particular combination of these with a default laghu length: e.g. RUPAKA TALAM comprises dhrutam + laghu, with a default laghu of 4 (CHATUSRA), giving a cycle length of 2+4=6 beats. Other laghu can be swapped in to create JATI variants: e.g. KHANDA-JATI RUPAKA switches rupaka's default 4-beat chatusra laghu for the 5-beat KHANDA laghu, extending the cycle to 2+5=7 beats.

This construction system, the SULADI SAPTA TALA, contains 7 talam, each with 5 jati options, a total of 35 cycles (*opposite top*). Other rhythms are used too: e.g. the famous 8-beat ADI TALAM (*lower opposite*), fabled to have echoed throughout the newborn universe during Lord Shiva's "tandav" dance of creation. Other construction systems also exist, such as the MELAKARTA (72 cycles) and the CHANDA (108 cycles).

Carnatic talam are typically elaborated on the double-headed mridangam drum, often supported by the ghatam clay pot, morsing jaw-harp, and tambourine-like kanjira. Musicians embody their grooves using the SOLKATTU system, counting the beats on the fingers and palms while "speaking" them using KONNAKOL, a set of drum-derived syllables: e.g. the 8 beats of adi talam (4+2+2 = chatusra laghu + dhrutam + dhrutam) may be tapped with the right hand striking the left palm:[1] palm clap, [2] pinky finger, [3] ring finger, [4] middle finger; [5] palm clap, [6] reverse clap; [7] palm clap, [8] reverse clap.

TALAM	FORMULA	JATI (i.e. LAGHU VARIANT USED)				
		Tisra (3)	Chatusra (4)	Khanda (5)	Misra (7)	Sankeerna (9)
Dhruva	L+D+L+L	11	**14**	17	23	29
Matya	L+D+L	8	10	12	16	20
Rupaka	D+L	5	**6**	7	9	11
Jhampa	L+A+D	6	7	8	**10**	12
Triputa	L+D+D	7	**8**	9	11	13
Ata	L+L+D+D	10	12	**14**	18	22
Eka	L	3	**4**	5	7	9

ABOVE: The SULADI SAPTA TALA: A=anudhrutam (1 beat), D=dhrutam (2 beats), L=laghu (3/4/5/7/9 beats). Each talam has a formula and a default laghu (circled), as well as four jati (variants), created by swapping in other laghu: e.g. jhampa (L+A+D) = misra laghu (7) + anudhrutam (1) + dhrutam (2) = 10.

1: 'Ta'
2: 'Ta-Ka'
3: 'Ta-Ki-Ta'
4: 'Ta-Ka-Di-Mi'
5: 'Ta-Di-Gi-Na-Ka'
8: 'Ta-Ka-Di-Mi Ta-Ka-Ju-Na'

LEFT: Basic KONNAKOL syllables. Other lengths and values can be formed by combining them (e.g. 7 as 3+2+2: "Ta-Ki-Ta, Ta-Ka, Ta-Ka"), or by inserting pauses (e.g. 7 as a stretched 5: "Ta-[-]-Di-[-]-Gi-Na-Ka"). These syllables are also used to 'slice up' individual beat units into different equal segments, a process known as 'nadai' (e.g. double-timing a 3-beat cycle as "Ta-Ka, Ta-Ka, Ta-Ka", then triple-timing it to "Ta-Ki-Ta, Ta-Ki-Ta, Ta-Ki-Ta", without changing tempo), e.g. see Adi Tala, BELOW.

ADI TALA 8 BEATS (4 + 2 + 2)							
1	2	3	4	5	6	7	8
FIRST SPEED							
TA	ka	di	mi	TA	ka	JU	no
SECOND SPEED							
TA ka	di mi	TA ka	ju no	TA ka	di mi	TA ka	ju no
THIRD SPEED							
TA ka di mi	TA ka ju no	TA ka di mi	TA ka ju no	TA ka di mi	TA ka ju no	TA ka di mi	TA ka ju no
VARIATION EXAMPLE							
TA	ka	di	mi	TA ka di mi TA ka ju no TA	ka	di mi	JU	no

Repetition & Variation
and irregular rhythm

REPETITION is fundamental to rhythm. Our brains thrive on finding patterns. That is why a good dance groove is repetitious, steady enough to feel solid, but intricate enough to continually delight. But VARIATION is also fundamental to music. After we figure out the puzzle, we want something new. Songwriters and composers struggle to find just the right combination of familiarity and excitement, comfort and challenge. In the opening measures of Mozart's *Eine Kleine Nachtmusik* (*below*), the lively **and 3** in the first measure is quickly followed by **and 1, and 2, and 3**, repeating the rhythmic figure but also building it up. It's theme and development within just two measures.

Sometimes, patterns are more subtle and elusive. We see the kinship of ocean waves even though no two are the same. RUBATO phrasing has beats, but allows phrases to speed up or slow down slightly, creating a flowing, breathing effect. A similar effect was achieved by impressionists like Claude Debussy, using subtle shifts in phrasing, and placing melodies off the beat, to create an unmetered floating feel.

Music in FREE RHYTHM has no regular beats. In the Zen-like spacious and serene music of Japanese SHAKUHACHI flute, striking phrases are followed with long pauses, making you focus equally on sound and silence, attending mindfully to the here and now. The rhythms of FREE JAZZ, by contrast, can seem uncontrolled and wild, but if you listen carefully, musicians often seem to be feeling a rhythm internally, and playing all around it rather than stating it overtly.

Mozart, EINE KLEINE NACHTMUSIK, *opening*, 1787

Opening phrase of WELL YOU NEEDN'T by Thelonious Monk, 1944

ABOVE: Jazz composer Thelonious Monk begins his 1944 song *Well You Needn't* with a catchy phrase, then builds the entire first section of the song from repetition and variation of this phrase. The second line slightly alters the melody, the third line is the same as the first. In the last line Monk hones in on the first four notes of the melody, "and 1 and 2," repeating them as "and 4 and 1." Your ear catches the coherence of the music, while being titillated by its transformations. Using just part of a phrase, "and 1 and 2", is **FRAGMENTATION**; moving its position, "and 4 and 1", is **DISPLACEMENT**.

Debussy, NUAGES mm. 5-8

LEFT: Debussy introduces the English horns in the middle of the first measure with three fast notes, then several longer notes without any apparent rhythmic pattern. Some of these float across the bar line (the curved TIE). In the first bar, clarinets and bassoons hold long notes from previous measures, and repeat this effect. But before they do, flutes and horns enter with similar long floaty overlapping notes.

Musical Form
larger movement in time

Rhythm does not only operate at the small scale of subdivisions, beats, and measures. Music also has larger structures that play out in time, and these too are a type of rhythm. Many folk songs consist of four-line verse after four-line verse. Somewhat larger groupings, of 8, 16, or 32 measures, are SECTIONS, and music based on them is SECTIONAL.

AABA is a sectional form common in both popular song and jazz. Typically, the first A section is followed by another with the same melody. The B section, or BRIDGE, has a new melody built on new chords. Then the final A returns. The most familiar blues form, TWELVE-BAR BLUES consists of three lines of four measures each. The first line sets out an idea, the second repeats it, and the last adds to it. Such repetition combined with variety allows musicians to express themselves.

The large-scale compositions of Western classical music (sonatas, concertos, symphonies) often follow a BEGINNING, MIDDLE, END structure (*lower, opposite*). Other traditions employ ACCUMULATIVE form, one long stretch with no clear sections, intertwined repetition and variation, that slowly build intensity. In religious traditions such as Sufi QAWWALI or Afrocuban LUCUMÍ, this type of experience can lead to religious ecstasy or trance. In classical Arabic music, musicians seek TARAB, aesthetic ecstasy, through imaginative improvisations.

Rhythm occurs throughout music, from the smallest subdivisions to the largest of forms, from driving grooves to gentle rubatos, from drums to strings to voices. There are endless creative rhythmic concepts in the world's musics; this small book could include only a few. Please keep on exploring.

A Verse 1. "Yesterday / All my troubles seemed so far away / ... / ..."
A Verse 2. "Suddenly / I'm not half the man I used to be / ... / ..."
B Bridge. "Why she had to go / I don't know ... / ... / ..."
A Verse 3. "Yesterday / Love was such an easy game to play / ... / ..."

YESTERDAY, Lennon-McCartney, 1965

ABOVE: *The AABA form. The first A section is an eight-bar verse. The second A follows with the same melody. The B section, or* BRIDGE, *is also eight bars, with a new melody built on new chords. Then the final A returns. As this form unfolds in time (its larger rhythm) the first two As establish and reinforce a mood, B provides an intriguing departure, and the last A is a satisfying return.*

| You can read my letter, | you can't read my mind | (instrumental ... | ...) |
  1   2   3   4

| You can read my letter, | you can't read my mind | (instrumental ... | ...) |
  1   2   3   4

| If you see me laughing, | I'm laughing just to keep from crying | (instrumental ... | ...) |
  1   2   3   4

YOU CAN READ MY LETTER, floating verse, *e.g. recorded by* Tommy McClennan, 1941

ABOVE: THE THREE-LINE BLUES FORM. *The situation set out in the first line is usually some sort of conflict, about love, sex, society or some other topic. The second line reinforces it. The third line might resolve the problem, or, as in the verse above, show it from another angle, intensifying it or adding a witty or sardonic comment. And then? This is blues, another problem is sure to follow.*

Sonata

EXPOSITION: Theme A / Transition / Theme B (often in a new key)

DEVELOPMENT: Themes A and B varied, and transposed to new keys

RECAPITULATION: Theme A / Transition / Theme B in the key of theme A

ABOVE: THE SONATA FORM *echoes the three-stage* BEGINNING-MIDDLE-END *narrative structure originally proposed by Aristotle. At the beginning themes are set out and counterthemes proposed. Next, the themes and counterthemes are developed, modulating through different keys. These middle sections are experienced as unstable and dangerous; through them the listener undergoes an emotional or spiritual journey. In the end the music returns to its home key, but the long experience of transformation, of difficulties overcome, has matured and deepened it.*

APPENDIX: WESTERN RHYTHMIC NOTATION